CHAPLAINCY LIBRARY

FICTION/HUMOUR

* Please return within two months *

SAINTS AND SINODS

... EMBLAZONED WITH HIS OR WITH HERS

SAINTS
AND SINODS

by S. J. FORREST

ILLUSTRATED BY
E. W. FORREST

MOWBRAYS
LONDON & OXFORD

© A. R. Mowbray & Co Ltd 1971

Printed in Great Britain by
Alden & Mowbray Ltd at the Alden Press, Oxford

SBN 264 64551 0

First published in 1971

DEDICATED

to my kindly old Mother
The Church of England,
one of the few bodies remaining on earth
still able to laugh at herself

S. John Forrest
Bournemouth
1971

.. THOUGHTS RUNNING INTO THE BRAIN

LIMERICK TIME

The dosage for limerick rhyme,
Is not more than seven at a time,
  One over the eight
  Is approaching a spate,
And a dozen a positive crime.

Yet limericks, when in the mood,
Unceasingly tend to exude,
  For when we're obsessed,
  There's no time for a rest,
For reading, or sleeping, or food.

Our sensitive ganglions hum
With the beat of a rhythmical drum,
  And whatever we do
  Is bewitched, through and through,
With a lum-tiddy, lum-tiddy, TUM!

The thoughts running into the brain,
With the speed of a non-stopping train,
　All follow so fast
　That each cancels the last,
And we scarcely can catch them again.

But sometimes it gets to the state
When they come at a murderous rate,
　And, in fear of the worst,
　In the shape of a burst,
We serve 'em all up on a plate.

All those we attempt to record,
In Mowbray's computers are stored,
　Till they're served in a book
　With a colourful look
At a price that we trust you afford.

... RESORTED TO TEAR-GAS AND GUNNERY

CLERGIMERICKS

Rev Riot

A chaplain, who preached in a nunnery,
Would break into verses, and punnery;
  Till the Mother Superior,
  To cope with hysteria,
Resorted to tear-gas and gunnery.

Copeless

The funny old bishop of Slope,
Is constantly losing his cope,
  For, his people at home
  Try to post it to Rome,
As a garment designed for a pope.

Anchored

A hermit, who grew a hibiscus.
With tentacles sticky and viscous,
  Was chagrined to own
  That it couldn't be shown,
Since he'd got it mixed up with his whiskers.

9

Nun Fun

Some nuns, in a mood of hilarity,
Have streamlined their customs, for clarity,
   With a crystallized prayer,
   And a minified wear
They are now called 'Transistors of Charity'.

Curvers

A clergyman, bold and audacious,
Said, 'Women, as servers, are gracious;
   For, men, at their prayers,
   Move in angles and squares,
But ladies are wholly curvaceous.'

Mitre Known

Said a burglar, who tended to gloat,
On stealing from people of note,
   'I earnestly wish,
   That when "doing" a bish,
It would not bring a lump to my throat.'

Tea Bags

A clergyman, modern and free
Now wears his pyjamas at tea;
   He will say, 'I'm agreed,
   That it's not in the Creed,
But I'm waiting for Vatican Three.'

... WEARS HIS PYJAMAS AT TEA

EMBLAZONED WITH HIS OR WITH HERS

BLUE STREAK

(Since the permission for women lay readers in the Church of England there has been much discussion on the appropriate garb to be worn when officiating.)

Oh Vicar, I cannot go reading tonight,
I haven't a thing I can wear!
My surplice no longer is whiter than white,
And I need a blue rinse in my hair;
My lay-reader's scarf is of last year's hue,
My cassock, a positive rogue!
I cannot perform till I've studied the norm,
In the 'Reader's Edition' of Vogue.

The unisex garment, supplied by the Church,
All discrimination deters,
Unless it's embroidered in legible script,
Emblazoned with HIS or with HERS;
The staircarpet scarf that we wear round the neck,
Is hardly an object of joy;
But surely it ought to be pink for a girl,
And blue in the case of a boy?

11

The Young Readers' Conference harps on the theme
Of the varying hem of the cassock:
The mini, or midi, which float in the air,
Or the maxi which trails on the hassock.
Our mighty cathedral, with elegant choir,
Is entranced by the gayest of sights:
The Lord Bishop's wife in her miniest robes,
And her sky-blue diocesan tights.

Though some like to dress in the guise of a man,
In places where Anglicans pray
Still more would uphold the feminine right
To remain ornamental and gay;
So the practice of modelling readers' robes
Could become quite a novel vocation,
As the corsetry firms find a part they can play
In the Church's newest foundation.

SEVEN DEADLY SYNODS

At the first deadly synod,
When all were yet untried,
The newly-elected candidates
Enjoyed a wave of PRIDE.

At the second deadly synod,
We now began to find,
A sense of ENVY, at the folks
Who didn't have the grind.

Financial discussions,
Which enveloped number three,
From elements of AVARICE,
Were not entirely free.

The fourth was well attended,
(We considered it a 'must'),
A totally dispassionate
Review of modern LUST.

At the fifth deadly synod,
All the guns began to fire,
In bursts of savage ANGER,
And in controversial ire.

B

At number six, the catering
Came up for fresh review,
And GLUTTONY was notable,
In speeches not a few.

For the seventh deadly synod,
It was hot, and we were loath
To toil, and thus surrendered
To a monumental SLOTH

For, in a sultry atmosphere,
The weary spirit faints,
And seeks the bed provided
By the Psalmist, for the saints.

... COMFORTABLE SEAT

NEVEREND REVEREND

Our reverend incumbent is ridiculously shy,
On meeting his parishioners he seems to petrify,
But once he's in the pulpit, he becomes a learned don,
And rambles on,
  And on and on,
    And on and on and on!

His flow of phraseology is fine as any Dean's,
Although we find it difficult to fathom what he means;
But, when he strikes an argument particularly sound,
He wanders round,
  And round and round,
    And round and round and round.

But those who understand him, and preserve an open eye,
Consider his morality is really very high,
As like a mighty Galahad, questing a noble Cup,
He leads them up,
  And up and up,
    And up and up and up.

His churchmanship, however, is unfathomably low,
(The Roman Church in Holland he considers rather slow!);
He scorns the Church's surplices, reverting to the gown,
While services go
    Down and down,
        And down and down and down.

His feeling for antiquity is notably complete,
Indeed his speciality is prehistoric Crete,
Of fine historic detail there is never any lack;
He takes his people
    Back and back,
        And back and back and back.

But, since the church was fitted with a comfortable seat,
We use the Vicar's sermons as a species of retreat,
We never try to rack our brains, or criticize or scoff,
But slumber off,
    And off and off,
        And off and off and off.

AMUESMENT ONLY

'Priests are asked to bring vestments, Amue and Cotta, Chasable, Tunide, a Cope.'
Twice-repeated advert. in a Church newspaper.

We couldn't believe it! Yet *twice* it repeated,
And still for the answer we grope,
This call to the clergy for Amue and Cotta,
For Chasable, Tunide, a Cope.

We've seen 'em in surplices, cassocks and collars,
We've seen pretty films of the Pope,
But never resplendent in Amue and Cotta,
In Chasable, Tunide, a Cope.

The Christian religion is richly inclusive,
Of infinite ranges and scope,
For picturesque clergy in Amue and Cotta,
In Chasable, Tunide, a Cope.

The churches should advertise, showing commercials,
Amid the detergents and soap,
Displaying their parsons in Amue and Cotta,
In Chasable, Tunide, a Cope.

And all who are weary of services dreary,
Or think that religion is dope,
Should seek out a pageant of Amue and Cotta,
Of Chasable, Tunide, a Cope.

For no one could damn you if wearing an Amue,
Or think you a soul without hope,
Or call you a rotta in Amue and Cotta,
In Chasable, Tunide, a Cope.

The star-eyed and moon-eyed could worship the Tunide,
And possibly long to elope,
With glamorous curates in Amue and Cotta,
In Chasable, Tunide, a Cope.

So one day in heaven we'll come to the vision,
Of radiant clerics, we hope,
Processing for ever in Amue and Cotta,
In Chasable, Tunide, a Cope.

CRANMER

ALTARATIONS

Although I'm Church of England,
I haven't been of late,
Since organized religion
Is somewhat out of date;
With desiccated clergy,
And fossil-forms of prayer,
Which fail to bring conviction,
Or lead us anywhere.
I never went to worship,
Since everybody said
The Church was quite outdated,
And almost wholly dead.
'Twas plain its aged structure
Was riddled with decay,
And in an early future
Would surely pass away.

I went to Church at Christmas,
In sentimental mood,
To rouse nostalgic echoes,
On bygone days to brood;
But horror rose on horror,
And left my mind deranged,
For services had altered,
And everything was changed!
The noble rites of Cranmer,
The fine old B.C.P.,
Had now been superseded,
As far as I could see;
A crowded congregation,
Equipped with books of blue,
Were ploughing through a service,
Described as 'Series Two'.

The rights of every voter
To find his Church the same,
Are cynically flouted
By such a Christmas game;
These words, so unfamiliar,
The language, stark and bare,
All blatantly unsuited
For Anglicans at prayer.
If changes thus continue,
We confidently state,
The Church of England structure
Will soon disintegrate;
As clergymen, and vandals,
Injure her soul unique,
And thus destroy for ever
A valuable antique.

DEMONSTRATE

DEMO KING

Our parson has a simple creed,
Exactly what the people need;
It's popular and up to date,
The bold commandment: DEMONSTRATE!

His teaching goes with such a swing,
We've labelled him the Demo King,
And follow, in a mighty spate,
As he rides forth to demonstrate.

A faith magnificently free
From all the old complexity,
That parsons used to preach and prate,
This vital call to demonstrate.

Let clergy talk their faces blue
On what is good and what is true,
We much prefer to activate,
To get outside and demonstrate.

It matters little what your spite,
Or if your views are wrong or right,
Whatever you abominate,
Hold banners high and demonstrate!

For, if the demonstrations thrive,
The Church is seen to be alive,
No longer in a dying state,
Incapable to demonstrate.

Get out your placards, then, with me,
For this is Christianity,
Crusading, urgently irate;
And yet it's *fun* to demonstrate!

So stick your grievance on a board,
And follow in a raging horde,
Throw in the modern churchman's weight,
And protest! Boycott! Demonstrate!

The sky-pie merchants waste our time,
Discoursing on the realms sublime,
For in an otherworldly state,
There won't be scope to demonstrate.

...A JAMPOT SUPREME

COLLAR SCHEME

'I have a brother-in-law who is a clergyman, and he can be two different people, whether he wears his dog collar or not.' Letter in Sunday Press.

Those keen ecumenicals, merging their borders,
Are wasting their time on the question of Orders;
For *now* we've discovered the source of validity,
Plainly defined with a perfect lucidity.

Now it is patently clear to the scholar,
That Clergyman-Power resides in the collar,
Which somehow imparts to the clerical station,
A characteristic transmogrification.

The specialist tailors, in secret researches,
Derived from the study of numberless churches,
Impart to these collars mysterious fluids
Obtained from the potions and herbs of the Druids.

Insidious liquors, by force esoteric,
Develop a serious mien in the cleric,
Restraining the wearer, by powerful laces,
From any desire to kick over the traces.

So long as his collar retains its connection,
Your parson is safe from surrounding infection;
Intact in a ring of secure insulation,
From every invasion of worldly temptation.

But, once he discards his symbolical collar,
He leaps from his gloom and emotional squalor;
Reveals himself ready for orgy and revel,
And even admits he's a bit of a devil.

And clergymen, loving permissive society,
Sample its ties in alarming variety,
Stick out their necks, with a fervour hysterical,
Seeking a yoke that is wholly unclerical.

So people nostalgic, who love pious gloom,
And want a religion that reeks of the tomb,
Should only accept with a worthy esteem,
The parson engulfed in a jampot supreme.

...THAT OLD FASHIONED HAT

PARODY REVISED

'You are old Father Oblong', the young curate said,
'And it's time that you learnt to do better;
Yet you're wearing that old-fashioned hat on your head,
Don't you think you should ban the biretta?'

  'You're a youth,' said the priest, 'and you've plenty of hair,
    An all too luxuriant crop,
    But when you grow ancient and feel the cold air,
    You'll be glad of a lid on the top!'

'You are old, Father Oblong' the youth said again,
'And I think it excessively odd,
That you criticize Synods, as merely a pain,
And not of the Kingdom of God.'

  'In the older assemblies, I've suffered of yore,
    And I've yearned for relief, or for lunch,
    So, why do you think they'll be less of a bore
    When we tie the whole lot in a bunch?'

'You are old, Father Oblong, yet surely agree
That our Church has an organization
Of model efficiency, technical, free,
With a total computerization.'

  'Of old,' said the Father, 'we did a good job,
    By visiting, preaching and prayer;
    No doubt, when you've ceased to behave like a yob,
    You will find that we had something there!'

DEBINGOED

'Vicar booed from bingo-hall', Newspaper.

In ancient days the heretics
Of every Western nation,
Were punished under heavy pains
Of excommunication;
In fear their clergy would denounce
Their spiritual sedition,
Or ferret out their private thoughts,
By cruel Inquisition.

But *now* it is the people's turn,
In days more democratic,
To excommunicate their priests
Of tendencies dogmatic;
A ghastly form of banishment,
Expressed in modern lingo,
By booing naughty clergymen
From sacred halls of Bingo.

. . . BANISHMENT

Cast from the social haunts of men,
In habitation frowzy,
These exiles solace broken hearts
With private housey-housey;
Or contemplate, in wistful mood,
A mythologic heaven,
Far from the scope of Kelly's eye,
Or cries of 'legs eleven'.

Let backward-looking popes beware
This grim debingoation,
And stick to harmless platitude
In every grand oration;
Lest through the journals of the world,
From Rome to San Domingo,
The banner-headlines blazon forth:
'THE POPE IS BANNED FROM BINGO.'

... DOLLYSERVS

SPYCHOPHANTY
(*after Lewis Carroll*)

'I would vastly prefer to have as a server a girl . . . rather than one of the cassock-creeping queers . . . with their "Yes, Father", and "No, Father", and all the rest of the unholy jargon.' Letter in *Church Times*.

'Twas snodmas[1] and the dollyservs
Did plip and chitter round the guss,[2]
All leggitty the minicurves
And the sacrisaints kerfuss.

'Beware the Spycophant, my wee,
The tongue that smarms, the eyes that leer;
Beware the dad-dad bird, and flee
The cassock-creeping queer!'

She took her maxi-blade in hand,
Long time her soapsome foe she sought,
Then rested she by the seeovee [3]
And stood awhile in thought.

[1] Probably the Festival of Synodical Government
[2] Meaning obscure; based perhaps on the initials G.S.S. (Green Shield Stamps?)
[3] Despite much research meaning remains impenetrable

And as in paislish thought she stood,
The Spychophant, with wax aflame,
Brast through the censerflecting wood,
And jargled as it came.

'One two, one two!' and through and through,
The maxi-blade swished left and right,
'Osiris won! Osiris too!,[4]
She chantled in delight.

'Twas snodmas and the dollyservs
Did plip and chitter in the guss,
All leggitty the minicurves,
And the sacrisaints kerfuss.

[4] May possibly refer to a mystery cult

CAT CULT

Concerning a certain ascetic,
We have a quaint story to tell:
He gives up his bed to a puss-cat,
In terror of going to hell.

He preaches a vital religion,
For convent, or suburb, or flat,
Derived from the ancient Egyptians,
The worship and cult of a cat.

The essence of true veneration,
Without any flurry or fuss,
Consists in the manifestation
Of deference due to the puss.

The morning devotions are simple:
He kneels to his fetish of silk,
And pours out an ample libation,
The cream of the cream of the milk.

C

Though fasts, in the Church, are discarded,
He yields up his fish and his meat,
Conserving it all for his goddess,
Ensuring her plenty to eat.

The granular foods, from the packet,
He likens to venial sin;
And views it a sacrilege mortal,
To feed a fine cat from a TIN!

A daily routine is essential,
To sweep out her lair with a broom,
Remembering always, with homage,
To rise when she enters the room.

The task of preparing the cushions,
Requires dedication and care:
Let worshippers stand to attention
Until she has chosen her chair!

Away with the vile unbeliever,
Who gives the first place to the dog!
Conferring with scorn on the feline,
The blasphemous title of 'Mog'.

Our Brother, secure in devotion,
Avers it is pleasing to find,
A faith with congenial purpose,
A goddess who knows her own mind.

... TRIP TO THE MOON

SAINTS AND SYNODS

Mortal Synod
If the Church *must* be governed synodically,
And ruled with a system, methodically,
  It might prove essential
  To trim its potential,
By shooting the lot periodically.

Faint Saints
The story is idle, we hope,
That the saints who were scrapped by the Pope,
  In bitter depression,
  And moody obsession,
Have taken to liquor and dope.

Holy Orbit
The girls of the parish all swoon
At the astronaut curate of Doone,
  So, the Church may enforce,
  In her ordinand's course,
A compulsory trip to the moon.

. . . HYMN NUMBAH CLICKETTY-CLICK

Quo Vadis?
An unsettled Churchman would sigh,
'To the Pope I'd be tempted to fly,
  But the things I deplore,
  On the Anglican shore,
Have all got to Rome before I.'

Silly Sheep
There was a young priest in the city,
Who said, 'In the Church it's a pity,
  Indeed, a disaster,
  They think the word "Pastor",
Refers to some kind of committee.'

Hymn Bored
Our staid congregation is sick
Of the bingo-mad vicar's new trick,
  His latest obsession,
  To start the procession
With, 'Hymn numbah clicketty-click!'

32

LOCO

In a small church in Oporto, a street-car passes through the sacristy leaving a wedge-shaped space for the priest's disrobing. (Guidebook.)

> Our Rector is a transport-fan,
> And frequently will talk,
> Of trams at Crich in Derbyshire,
> Or railway trains at York.
>
> But, since he's been to Portugal,
> In old Oporto town,
> That tramcar through a sacristy,
> Has really got him down!
>
> So now he's laid a railway line,
> For almost half a mile,
> Which tunnels underneath the crypt,
> And up the centre aisle.

BY SKI-LIFT...

And as this ardent transport-cult
Becomes a grand obsession,
He plans to run a trolley-bus
In every church procession.

A flying telpher-span, he thinks,
Would not be out of place,
Along the vast triforium,
And through the tower-space.

By ski-lift we shall scale the spire,
With strains of music soft;
Ascending by funicular,
To gain the organ loft.

Amid the grand memorials,
Decking the church, inside,
You'll find a marble monument
To Bradshaw's railway guide.

The Rector's built a signal-box
For reading the epistle,
And starts the choir and organist
With flag and railway-whistle.

He claims religion must become
A signal, shining bright,
And ancient gothic arches ring
With transports of delight.

...WISDOM DIVINE

WINE NOT?

A Catholic gourmet would say,
That it's always effective to pray
    For a wisdom divine
    On the subject of wine,
To St. Anthony Mary Claret.

Now, should the above be denounced,
By critics, and cruelly trounced,
    Who will carpingly say
    That this isn't the way
That St. Anthony's name is pronounced:

Then, no oenophile ought to forget,
As he looks on the wine when it's wet,
    To seek unafraid,
    The invisible aid,
Of St. Anthony Mary Claret.

EGIDIUS OR GILES

I wish I were Egidius,
Egidius, or Giles,
And clear from all wegidius
Wegidius, or wiles;
Untouched by sly eguidius,
Free from ignoble guiles,
And other foes perfidious,
Ensnaring or insidious,
    Listed in heaven's efidius,
    Efidius, or files.

If I could be Egidius,
A title all esmidius,
Esmidius or smiles,
With exclamations hideous,
I'd dance for long emidius,
And leap upon the etidius,
Upon the ceiling tiles!

DISGUISES HERSELF AS A RABBIT

ARTS AND CRAFTS

Maja Vestida
A Puritan, fuming and oathing,
Denounced every woman, with loathing,
　For it made him feel mad,
　That howe'er they were clad,
They were naked all under their clothing.

Titianus—Fecit-Fecit
A picture of ancient commission,
Was sternly refused exhibition,
　Till a chap, with a cold,
　Said, 'You ought to be told,
It's a Titian, a Titian a Titian!'

Bunny Nun
Our volatile deaconess Babbitt,
Disguises herself as a rabbit,
　'For', she says, 'it is fun,
　And they think I'm a nun,
In a Vatican-modernized habit.'

37

...BY MEANS OF A BLOW-LAMP AND SCRAPERS

Show a Leg
A bishop, who read in the papers,
The latest sartorial capers,
   Was found, somewhat later,
   Removing each gaiter,
By means of a blow-lamp and scrapers.

Spring Tidy
The Annual Spring-Clean of my den,
A nightmare abhorrent to men,
   Starts a feverish chase,
   Not a thing can I trace
Till I get it untidy again!

Spirited

A preacher, involved in perplexity
With notes of excessive convexity,
  Discovered it handy
  To soak them in brandy;
Which gave them transparent perspexity.

Art Trouble

A clerical artist of Chart,
Was crushed by his output of art,
  For, he said, 'I adore
  All my work, more and more,
And we don't find it easy to part.'

... SOAK THEM IN BRANDY

...TRIED TO KEEP IT PRIVATE

OPEN SPACE

The verdict: 'Phalacrosis',
That's what the doctor said:
A serious infection
Which had risen to my head.
The state was quite intractable,
He made this wholly clear,
With calm and icy utterance
That turned me very queer.
I thought to keep it private,
But a secret gets around
My friends and my acquaintances
Took fright and went to ground.
The nature of the ailment
To enquire I didn't dare,
Lest it should overwhelm me
With a terminal despair.
Yet, people reminiscent
Of the comforters of Job,
Are never very distant
On this miserable globe!
They helpfully informed me
With a sympathetic sigh,
That phalacrotic sufferers
Eventually die.

This malady incurable,
Evading all research
Is rife among professionals
Especially the Church.
The more I tried escaping it,
The more I seemed to learn,
And like a hunted animal,
Had nowhere I could turn.
I toyed with euthanasia,
In fear of final pain,
And thoughts of reckless suicide
Were reeling through my brain.

To quell my surging fantasies,
Samaritans were called,
Who murmured, 'Phalacrosis!
All *that* means is—going bald.'

... BY SOME INDUCTION RITE

WORSE HALF

'The only thing about your new incumbent that I don't like is the fact that he is not married: so come on girls, and get him married off!' Diocesan Bishop at an Induction.

We cannot trust our clergyman,
The reason must be said:
Although he's quite a pleasant chap,
He still remains unwed!

His romanizing practices
We've learnt to tolerate,
If only he would not attempt
To ape the celibate.

For, in our homely English Church,
The essence of its life
Is not within the clergyman,
But in the Vicar's wife.

And, when the bishops come to church,
Our ministry to bless,
They should, by some induction-rite,
Instal the Vicaress.

Our with-it Prelate now projects
A nationwide crusade,
Enlisting every dolly-bird,
And eligible maid:

A raid upon all ministers
Who fear to wed, or scoff
At matrimonial urgency,
And get them married off!

And, when all England's parishes
Are purged of celibates,
They'll turn upon the monasteries,
And storm their ancient gates.

The frightened monks of Mirfield, Yorks.,
Are storing armament;
While Kelham is commissioning
An Ark upon the Trent.

At Cowley, they are studying,
In monumental fear,
An old Tibetan treatise
On the means to disappear.

But Nashdom monks alone remain
In confidence immersed,
Assured that good St. Benedict
Will see them through the worst!

Yet, all alert Diocesans,
Who seek a vital staff,
Will give their priests no quarter,
Till they find a Better Half!

ON THE SCENT

Religion from the Aerosol,
Is quite a new conceit,
To save the Church from verbiage
Entirely obsolete;
When faith and hope and charity
Are mixed with perfumes gay
And all the Vicar needs to do
Is murmur, 'Let us spray.'

Those incense-burning thuribles
Are very nearly dead;
So methods technological
Are utilized instead,
Creating thus an atmosphere
To aid the simple prayer,
With modern thurif-aerosols,
That sanctify the air.

The aerosol of Penitence,
Has yet to be fulfilled;
But essences of Happiness
Are readily distilled;
The scent of Generosity
Has also found a spray,
At festivals of Stewardship,
And even Easter Day!

For meetings ecumenical
The aerosol is fine,
Diffusing clouds of fellowship,
And brotherhood divine;
Though, sometimes one may criticize
The emotional intent,
Complaining that the sentiment
Was not the scent he meant.

So now we learn to vaporize
The antidotes of Sin,
By pressurized diffusion
From a neat and handy tin;
Thus Charity is aerosoled,
To each and every man,
And, sweetly odoriferous,
We practise what we can.

THE CORPORATION MUCK-CART

POLLUTANT

'Too many people on one spot may become the most serious pollutants of all.' Speaker on the Pollution problem.

The good old Bishop Heber,
On Java's spicy isle,
Where 'every prospect pleases,
And only man is vile,'
Now joins his hands with Calvin
On man's depravity,
In crying, 'This we told you,
And we were right you see!'

For Man, of noble reason,
So infinite in scope,
Angelic in his bearing,
And godlike in his hope;
This paragon of beauty,
Is now displayed in worth
As merely a pollutant
Who clutters up the earth.

Our literature and drama,
And brash permissive art,
The anarchistic teachings
Which from all goodness part,
Combine in bearing witness
Enough to make us weep,
And prove this erring cosmos
A putrid refuse-heap.

Yet can we reach salvation,
Or overcome our hurt,
While classed as mere pollutants,
Or stigmatized as dirt?
A fairer, nobler image
Of Man must needs be shewn,
The corporation muck-cart,
Is *not* his natural throne!

TICKLED PINK

Poor Rosie suffered a hideous fright
As crooks broke into her home at night;
As a burglar fled on her favourite bike,
She decided to purchase a bloodthirsty tyke.
So she sought for a thoroughly villainous hound
And returned with the wickedest cur she found:
But she'd hardly got him across the Square,
When he rolled on his back, with his legs in the air.

> *Rosie, Rosie, tickle me Rosie,*
> *Tickle my tummy and tickle my toesie,*
> *Tickle my ears and tickle my nosie*
> *Tickle me dumb, tickle me dozy!*

Rosie protested: 'But this isn't right,
I needed a watchdog to snarl and to bite,
I needed a monster, with slavering jaws,
With a tiger's teeth and enormous claws,
I needed a Cerberus, breathing out fire,
With a bark like the shout of the old town crier,
I wanted a hound with a devil inside.'
But the old doggie rolled in the dirt and cried:

> *Rosie, Rosie, tickle me Rosie,*
> *Tickle my tummy and tickle my toesie,*
> *Tickle my ears and tickle my nosie,*
> *Tickle me dumb, and tickle me dozy*

Rosie fed him on curry and fire,
She dosed him with tin-tacks to generate ire,
She glared in his eyes with implacable looks,
And taught him to chew London telephone-books;
She tried to be fierce, and she tried to be strong,
But still the old reprobate took it all wrong,
And the tiniest twinkle that gleamed in her eye
Made the silly old thing roll over and cry:

> *Rosie, Rosie, tickle me Rosie,*
> *Tickle my tummy and tickle my toesie,*
> *Tickle my ears and tickle my nosie*
> *Tickle me dumb, and tickle me dozy!*

One night there arrived a most villainous tough,
Determined to carry off Rosie's stuff,
So he climbed in the yard and he broke in the shed,
And there he encountered the old dog Fred:
Who promptly forgot both his bark and his bite,
In the hope of a game on a lonesome night;
As he rolled on the floor, with his legs in the air
And faithfully uttered his favourite prayer:

Rosie, Rosie, tickle me Rosie,
Tickle my tummy, and tickle my toesie,
Tickle my ears and tickle my nosie,
Tickle me dumb, and tickle me dozy!

Now the tough old crook had a gentle mind,
And to sloppy old dogs he was never unkind,
So he stooped and he tickled with might and main,
Repeating the process again and again;
A sport that continued a long, long time,
Till the cops could be called to the scene of the crime,
And the constable came and the man was nicked:
But the old hound sang as the handcuffs clicked:

Rosie, Rosie, tickle me Rosie,
Tickle my tummy and tickle my toesie,
Tickle my ears and tickle my nosie,
Tickle me dumb, and tickle me dozy!

Dogged

There was a grim cleric, who said,
'Now the dog-collar seems to be dead,
  As a means to atone,
  I shall feed on a bone
And dwell in a kennel, instead.'

Liverish

There was a French lady, whose *foie*,
Behaved like a *je ne sais quoi*,
  Till she cried, 'Though my blood
  Is as turgid as mud,
I couldn't say *boue* to a *oie*.'

Pastiche

A poet, defective on sonics,
When wearied with potions and tonics,
  Consumed vermicelli
  And tagliatelli,
To stimulate sound macaronics.

... DWELL IN A KENNEL

... MILITANT FIGHTER

Rhymeless Reason
A soldier, from Sugar Loaf Rock,
Succeeded in scoring a bulls-eye,
  But he drew a firm line
  At a corporal's stripe,
'For', he said, 'I should feel such a humbug.'

Rick Trick
A clergyman-farmer from Limerick
Was moved, on occasion, to hymn a rick,
  He fashioned his verse
  In Gaelic and Erse,
And, what he absurdly called, Cymeric.

Hard Head
A bishop, who daily grows brighter
Has lately discarded his mitre.
  Now he wears, like a pelmet,
  A soldier's tin helmet:
'The sign of a militant fighter!'

THE CHURCHYARD DONKEY

BLACKER THAN WHITE

I never loved philosophy,
Preferring simple mirth,
But now, at last I've thunk a thought
Which ought to change the earth!

Some learned etymologists
Emphatically teach
That, from the Anglo-Saxon 'blac',[1]
We take our word for 'bleach':

Detergent manufacturers
May boggle at the sight,
Yet, here we have the standing proof,
TO SHOW THAT BLACK IS WHITE!

This logic swells my head with pride,
My brain has grown so fat,
I feel the pressure on my brows
Is bursting through my hat.

[1] or *blaec*

A hat already damaged,
And of seemliness bereft;
I've eaten it so frequently
There's hardly any left!

Seeking a gentle audience,
I only found an ass:
The churchyard donkey, which we keep
To crop the roughest grass.

Into his kind and ample ear
(He couldn't carp or scoff),
I talked and talked until at last,
His hind-leg tumbled off.

I argued on and on, enough
To fill a massive tome,
Till all the air was filled with 'Moo',
The cows had all come home!

Let critics scowl with blackest glare,
And call my verses trite;
I face them all in cheerful heart,
Knowing that BLACK IS WHITE!